Copyright © 2018 Tekkan
Artwork Copyright © 2018

All rights reserved.
First Printing, 2018
ISBN 978-1-7324107-2-5

To contact Tekkan please email:
buddhaboy1289@gmail.com

Table of Contents

Asphalt Driveway Co................................ Page 1

Shakespeare and Zen .... Page 13

Scootering in Kyoto .... Page 21

Continents .... Page 36

Philadelphia .... Page 50

Cottonwood Poems .... Page 55

Politics ....Page 65

Myths and Dreams .... Page 83

Indra's Net .... Page 94

Heart Sutra .... Page 98

How to Read My Poems

I have married the sonnet to the tanka. I tell a story in the sonnet — using three quatrains, separated by line spaces, and a final couplet. The story builds to a conclusion in the couplet. The tanka is a commentary, or a counterpoint, to the sonnet — the combined poems have two endings.

I don't rhyme my sonnets, because I want freer expression. I want to be direct in my meaning — I want people to clearly understand my meaning. The metaphors are inspired by Shakespeare, and the (aimed-for) precision is in imitation of Japanese style. Using the sonnet with the tanka, I am mixing the sensibility of the Occident and the Orient — which I have done by living in England, Japan, and America.

I don't punctuate much in my poetry. I want the words themselves to do the work. There is logic between words, and the forms provide structure. By not using punctuation I hope to direct readers to carefully attend to each word — to appreciate the graininess of words.

Reading my poems silently, say, on a bus, a train, or an airplane, and reading them aloud, may be different experiences. The way I've written there's not always a pause intended at the end of the line. Hint: *My poems are to be recited not as lines, but as phrases, and a phrase often overflows the break at the end of a line. I pause and take a breath where it seems natural for me to pause. Another person may pause differently than I do.*

Each single poem is a piece of a mosaic, and it is my hope that the collection of poems form an accurate portrait of consciousness.

My daughter, Jocelyn MacDonald, is a wonderful artist. Her art work graces this book.

I am Barry MacDonald. I received the *dharma* name, *Tekkan*, which means, Iron Man, a settled practitioner of great determination.

— *Tekkan*

Everyday Mind III

Asphalt Driveway Co.

I was lucky years ago to work on
The crews that put in asphalt driveways in
The summer and we came in tall trucks with
A tractor a roller and a paver

And we were young men exercising our strength
And honing our skills and learning what was
Necessary — like standing on a load
Of asphalt while the soles of our boots burned

And shoveling from the truck down into
A wheelbarrow because that is the
Only way to get the asphalt to an
Odd place — there was no use in wearing

Gloves because they would be worn out very
Fast so our hands developed calluses.

I used a maul
a shovel
and a pickax
and grew a
capacious heart.

Willie's appearance might not impress you
Because he was too thin and tanned almost
Black and the sun is not kind to exposed
Skin — he was silent unpredictable

And volatile — but as the chief on an
Asphalt driveway crew he was a master
Craftsman working from his tractor seat at
Timing the arrivals of the trucks and

The moving of the grunts and at tearing
Out the old driveway and sculpting the ground
With an eye for the drainage of water
And he was good at raking stones into

Place and once the asphalt was flowing he
Knew how to lay an impeccable mat.

Willie was wicked
in his rages over
carelessness or
stupidity or
for no reason.

Grunts

Davey folded the six plastic rings that
Connected a six-pack of pop into
A single ring and with his hands grasping
Behind his neck he tore it apart and

Joey franticly shoveled the stones
In the correct general direction
And Joey drove hastily weaving
Around the traffic with a hot load of

Asphalt and there came a day I had to
Prove myself so I swung a pickax like
John Henry and the next day they let a
Surplus guy go and kept me and with my

Boot I balanced on an empty pop can
And with my fingers tapping crushed the can.

The crew chief mastered
all the necessary skills
and he sits in the
tractor seat and he
determines everything.

A tamper is a steel pole with a square
Ending that is used to put a raised edge
Alongside an asphalt driveway and I
I had a good eye for tamping a straight

Line and the chiefs selected me because
My tamping was a fine finishing touch
And I was happy because I could keep
Working and I had a skill setting me

Apart and I enjoyed riding to jobs
In the back of a tall dump truck wearing
A bandana but not a shirt feeling
Like a pirate and encountering the

Curious expressions of passersby
Because I was a member of the crew.

It is easy to
encourage a young man
and entice him to
work like a raging demon —
give him some belonging.

A roller uses two cylinder wheels
That we filled with water and it's about
Twice as big as a golf cart and I went
Forward by pushing a lever forward

And backward the same way and one day I
Was rolling pressing a just laid driveway
Going right to the edge of a ten foot
Drop enjoying an easy interlude

Between hard labor and I pulled back on
The lever but the roller kept on so
I jumped and down it went boom boom and like
A cat I landed with my heart going

Boom boom and I might have been dozing a
Little beforehand but then I woke up.

Synchronicity —
a mechanical failure
a ten foot drop and
vigorous dexterity
produced a happy ending.

It was a joke we enjoyed — four of the
State government road crew were leaning on
Their shovels as one was shoveling — though
There might have been a little envy too

Because we were like skinny feral cats —
And from the moment we arrived at the
Yard there was ceaseless motion before dawn
And through the heat of summer days until

Returning past the evening twilight and
The only occasional rest was if
There was room for me in the cab to doze
On the way to the next job otherwise

I'd stand in the dumpster part of the truck
With my arms over the sides holding on.

Such a test of pride —
to lift a wheelbarrow
and hurl it up and
over the side into the
dump truck about ten feet high.

A paver connects to a dump truck as
The steel form the asphalt flows into when
The load is raised and it lays the mat and
There's a place for the novice grunts to stand

And stir the asphalt to the corners with
A shovel and because the paver is often
Not as wide as necessary and as
Constancy and speed are needed the

Grunt must fling shovelfuls accurately
And hastily until the job is done —
With the asphalt steaming and under the
Sun blazing if the new guys made it through

The day and if they could return to the
Yard the next morning they could work again.

The labor absorbs
attention so there's no time
beyond shovelfuls
beyond the immediate
calling for utmost effort.

There was a job in the open country
On a hilltop with a glorious view
And we prepared the ground for a lengthy
Driveway on a cool morning tearing out

The old asphalt with the maul shovels and
The tractor and when the earth was smoothed we
Spread the underlying stones with shovels
And rakes and there's an art to seeing the

High and low places and spreading smoothly
And as we were working sporadically
And then attentively we noticed the
Clouds becoming dark anticipating

Rain and it cheered our hearts at the prospect
Of honorably working half the day.

Our hearts jumped with the
prospect of lucky freedom
from a day's labor
as children playing hooky
who are blameless and shameless.

"You are really good at taking shit" said
Steve who was on the way to becoming
A chief and I was puzzled as every
Grunt took abuse from Willie and why should

I take anything personally? I
Could do the work was paying for college
And was Steve complimenting? I don't know —
Summers later near the ending of a

Day some kids were laughing at me because
I could hardly stand — I was five-foot-two
And I looked like a kid — and Carrie our
Chief told them to shut up and they did — and

I was grateful because I was doing
Good work and had earned everyone's respect.

In Oxford England
the university dons
and the students weren't
exchanging profanity —
they didn't know hard labor.

I was nearing the end of my time on
The crews and I had chosen not to drive
The trucks as I saw difficulty that
Might threaten my job so I stayed a grunt

Those summers and they knew I was going
To college but not to Oxford England
The final year and I didn't tell them
Because some might have made it harder for

Me — or not I don't know — but once Willie
Had an easy day sealcoating — which meant
Pushing a broom — and he chose me to go
Because he knew I was leaving and he

Let me sleep in the cab between jobs and
So we had the easiest day ever.

And then Willie said
I would tell my grandchildren
about him and me
about summers of hard work
about this one easy day.

Escape

Upon my arrival at Oxford and
St. Michael's Hall for a year of study
Hearing the pealing bells in the morning
I thought of the guys lining up in the

Yard in the three crews before dawn ready
For a day of hard labor and I was
Grateful for the rich experience of
Putting in driveways paying my own way

Discovering "culture" and mixing with
A more refined sort of people with whom my
Words had to be weighed carefully before
I spoke — and today I'm very grateful

To have known wrenching metamorphosis
And to have tasted whole-hearted effort.

I am grateful
to know the capacity
the precision and
and the talent required
to control a tractor's blade.

John Henry

Another morning sun will sear the air —
Such humidity. The whole body aches.
To rise again to labor hard will tear
Muscles from sinews. The tired body quakes.
Shades don't cool the blazing of the noon sun.
Within a soul a fury wakes to coil
A wrath to hurl the maul to powder tons
Of stone to hide a shame in deadly toil.
Evening glows with the grace of sunset's rose.
At twilight the sweat dries in salty cakes
Across those huge slumped shoulders and he dozes
As he stumbles as he trudges as he aches.
He dreams of mountains cold rivers and lakes —
The earth is so beautiful that he aches.

Shakespeare and Zen

While waiting for a train in Amsterdam
While traveling as an American
And sensing the depth of history and
Culture of Europe while reading Shakespeare's

Sonnets I was filled with admiration
Because I loved the way he weighed the words
Within a line for resonation and
How the meaning flowed and turned and how the

Florid language presented the world with
The lens of Elizabethan England
And so I acquired a direction
But admiration and ability

Are different and I required years
To distill a healthy emulation.

But I must comment
on the crazy rhyming scheme
of Shakespeare's sonnets —
I don't see the need to do
a Houdini trick with words.

Hosshinji — a Zen Temple in Japan

Somewhere Sometime long ago someone did
Discover the pleasing impact of a
Bell and leave it to the Japanese to
Refine a practice to perfect the

Forging to house it by itself at a
Buddhist temple and to swing a pole and
Strike it in the morning at noon and in
The evening and thereby mark the day with

Sound and if you stand nearby your inner
Ears will feel the pressures and the waves of
Reverberating air and for me I'm
Led to joyful solemnity as the

Tone seems to pierce my heart with knowledge as
I recognize such unearthly beauty.

As the bell is a
summons to remember
the wondrous gift of
life so I remember my
intentions and am grateful.

Some of the monks wanted the title priest
And others wanted the perfection of
Wisdom the wisdom arising before
Knowledge and once a practice period

Began the temple was revealed as
It is — an ancient stream — and an air of
Seriousness settled among us and
The slightest harmonious gesture could

Contribute to the merging of effort
With bells rituals and meditation
With a peculiar focus — to study
The moment as it emerges without

Flinching calmly sitting without motion
Allowing whatever there is to come.

Taking the time and
becoming quiet and making
effortless effort
simply paying attention
and letting mind waves ripple.

There were stone steps to the cemetery
And there was a bamboo fence alongside
And I had a spot overlooking the
Temple grounds where I went between sittings

Of meditation and I was taken
By more than just the tile roofs the garden the
Bell tower and smoke from the kitchen
Pipe as I sat on a step pursuing

Just the right posture of mind desiring
The way to extinguish desires and by
The third day maintaining a straight back was
Difficult but by the fifth every ache

Vanished and sitting quietly was a
Joy and each moment an exploration.

Desiring to
extinguish desires is
paradoxical
somehow something has to
disappear and emerge.

When the practice period was done and
The air of seriousness lifted from
The temple before the visitors would
Leave Zen Master Harada raised a staff

And struck the tatami and said if we
Practiced wholeheartedly understanding
Enlightenment is as easy as the
Staff hitting the ground and we couldn't miss

And I remember Master Harada
The presenter of puzzles professing
To be pointing directly at the truth
And some thirty years later I'm still

Enchanted and mystified and pursuing
The posture of mind for liberation.

If impatient be
impatient and if fearful
be fearful he said
In the darkness there is light
In the light there is darkness.

Clouds in Water — a Zen Temple in America

I'm attuned to a joy arising as
I sit quietly with my legs crossed as
I listen as the teacher says thinking
I will live and die is only a way

Of believing I needn't be caught by
And though the idea is not new to
Me that I would feel a joy arising
As I entered a temple again and

I'm welcomed to the sanga again and
I'm immersed again in the presence of
The dharma and and I realize it's
Not about the joy arising as joy

Is transient but it is about the
Joy arising pointing a direction.

Because I've found
the capability
to be at home with
to be harmonized within
to be poised in the moment.

I love a gloomy day with a humid
Overcast sky just on the verge of rain
Because I declare my independence
From circumstances because I know gloom

Is a state of mind I don't have to live
With because I have learned to be quiet
To let thought dissipate and to allow
Emotion to pass without becoming

Disturbed and when I understand beneath
The veneer of thought and beyond the snares
Of circumstances and regardless of
Wounds I know it's possible in the midst

Of gloom to become awake attentive
Savoring the unexplainable peace.

The mind is only
a lens I use to see with —
it's untrustworthy
and easily disrupted
so I practice letting go.

Light and leaf — sun and sky — mind and sky — with
My eyes open I see the natural
Cooperation composing this world
And I wonder at the magic of it

That my skin absorbs the light just as a
Leaf absorbs the light just as the sun fills
The space surrounding the earth with light and
Somehow turns it blue and have you noticed

How we live subject to the natural
Drama of the sky ceaselessly moving
With clouds and rain and wind and light and have
You noticed how the mind ceaselessly moves

From happiness to discouragement to
Confusion and also astonishment?

Too seldom do I see
too infrequently notice
the churning magic
composing combinations
and ceaseless transformation.

Scootering in Kyoto

I bought a motorcycle but didn't
Know how to drive it so I got up at
3:00 a.m. and pushed it to an empty
Parking lot and resolved that I would do

One thousand starts and stops and acquire
The skill of hand pressure releasing the
Clutch while shifting with my foot all the while
Balancing precariously on tip

Toes as the bike was too tall for me and
Through several dark mornings my awkwardness
And terror diminished enough for me
To rumble to a gas station where the

Japanese attendant scrutinized me
Suspiciously — I must have looked nervous.

I was evading
rigorous regulation
as an outsider
as an American who
had more courage than good sense.

Before I got my bearings — before Zen —
I found myself on a motorcycle
One day ascending a winding mountain
Road following a dump truck and nothing

Spoils a ride more so I followed closely
Every turn balanced for the spurt of speed
To pass and I was poised and swerving right
And left leaning on the edge of the tires

Looking for seconds of clear straight road and
Today I don't remember passing or
Any detail of the ride afterwards
Except the frustration and the foolish

Exhilaration — I wasn't thinking
But I was imposing a solution.

Sitting quietly just
dwelling within energy —
I don't have to see
I don't have to think about
anything to be at peace.

On holidays the roads out of town were
Clogged for dozens of kilometers and
The Japanese were stuck motionless in
Their cars while I glided by on a strip

Of the road and whether on holiday
Or taking a day off I sometimes drove
My motorcycle across the island
To the Sea of Japan because I felt

An urge to go and with open roads I
Flew and with traffic I went carefully
But when arriving at the bay and the
Beach I took off my helmet and sat on a

Bench watching the undulating ocean
Pretending to have a point in coming.

I could navigate
I could go fast or slowly
but I didn't know
how to find satisfaction
or what to do with myself.

When a Western guy becomes an English
Teacher in the private schools that offer
Lessons one to one or several to one
It's easy for him to acquire a

Romeo complex because so many
Young Japanese women come hanging on
Every word and it's just like directing
Obedient flowers with syllables

And the women are usually much
More conversant than the salary men
From Mitsubishi who are traveling
To America who mumble and sweat

Who require the utmost attention
Who remind the teacher he is working.

Romeo needs a
modern-day stallion and
a motorcycle
serves wonderfully because
she goes behind holding on.

The sidewalks and alleys of downtown were
Quite littered with parked motorcycles and
Scooters and twice I found a device on
My tire I could only have removed by

Having a talk with the police as they
Wanted a fine occasionally and
They examined my international
Motorcycle license but couldn't know

It wasn't valid (though they held me once
Awhile) so fear and conscience impelled me
To trade the motorbike for a scooter —
Not requiring a motorcycle

License — and I discovered how lithe a
Scooter is and I became enchanted.

There's no shifting or
clutch just a turning of the
wrist and the scooter
zooms away maneuvering
like a swallow in the air.

I drove a motorcycle fast in those
First years across the island over the
Winding mountain roads through villages with
Thatched roofs and swift rivers pushing myself

At top speed in anticipation of
A week of Zen at *Hosshinji* in the
Town of Obama but as years passed
And my daily practice progressed I gave

Up the motor bike for a cub scooter
Designed for delivering newspapers
And it took me a lot longer to get to
The temple but I enjoyed the trip —

It's much better to linger on the edge
Of mysteries I'd like to penetrate.

An excited heart
and surging blood doesn't lead
to enlightenment —
I had to go slower to
cultivate understanding.

A scooter is insubstantial in weight
And size and can turn in a circle quite
Easily and though they aren't designed for
Highway speeds they accelerate quickly

So while sitting upright and turning my
Wrist forward I zoomed off pretending I
Was riding a magic carpet and each
Ride was an adventure dodging between

The dump trucks with paintings of samurai
Warriors with bulging eyes and busses
And taxis that could stop suddenly so
I often felt like a fly flitting by

Elephants careening down the narrow
Streets of Kyoto with my eyes open.

It's Japanese law
riders must wear helmets and
we looked so silly
on the miniscule scooters —
like insects with swollen heads.

Kyoto is densely populated and
I loved my scooter because I could scoot
By the dump trucks the taxis and the cars
As they were clogged on the streets and who wants

To be squeezed like sardines in a bus and
There's no faster way around town and I
Stayed off the congested routes and zipped past
My favorite temple for encouragement

And I liked to see the tile roofs and the
Wooden gates of traditional homes and
The Japanese are best at constructing
Ornamental walls in a pleasing style —

Things are carefully placed in Japan and
Quiet seclusion is harmonious.

Japanese don't mind
bumping each other on the
sidewalks as they are
crowded together but they
are mindful of boundaries.

As a teacher at Berlitz which charged a
Lot of money for English lessons
I was expected to be at school on
Time or else — so I couldn't be late — but

I had a hard head and consequences
Began to weigh on me only in the
Last minutes and I had a habit of
Leaving in a rush with not enough time

So I used the narrow strip of road by
The curb to bypass congested traffic
And I maneuvered with the urgency
Of a fool who hasn't learned his lesson —

Speeding on a scooter is risky and
Forgetting the time is regrettable.

My necktie flowed with
the wind and my eyes opened
with urgency as
yet again I had to go
as speedy as possible.

It's a youthful thing and requires spry
Ability with a good sense of timing
To drive a scooter in Kyoto as not
Much dignity accrues to bouncing and

Weaving along playing cat and mouse with
Truck and taxi drivers who thought we were
Nuisances while I abominated
Taxis because they stopped capriciously

With their automatic doors popping out
Suddenly — I wasn't deceived by their
White gloves — they assumed proprietary
Rights to the roads and were savages and

Yet I knew every thought qualifies as
Zen practice and harmony is the way.

It's a question of
preparation attitude
poise — leaving early
I didn't have to hurry
so I didn't get flustered.

I was like a water bug gliding on
The surface of a culture different
From America teaching English to
One or a few Japanese students

In small rooms and everyday I rode my
Scooter on the roads serving as the veins
For the body of their society
And there was much we didn't understand

About each other and my scooter was
So insubstantial nothing divided us
Except ways of thinking as contrasting
As night and day but I discovered Zen —

I came to pursue the original
Mystery — the wisdom before knowledge.

Everyday passing
the Kabuki theater
I couldn't grasp its
refined significances
but believe they are worthy.

After a number of years exploring
The various routes and destinations
Kyoto became homely — no matter what
The Japanese thought of me — because I

Became familiar with the bumps and turns
The temples and pachinko parlors and
The bridges over the Kamo River
And in the humidity of summer

Cicadas thrilled and in the winter I
Bundled up and in the rainy season
I wore rubber boots and a poncho and
Everyday I sat on my scooter

Exposed to the elements scooting on
The streets circulating within Kyoto.

I was passing by
impenetrable
mysteries as an
outsider who was learning
to be home in the moment.

I returned from *Hosshinji* after days
Of meditation and was scootering
In Kyoto when I was caught by a fool
In a Mercedes Benz who was blowing

His horn and careening through traffic who
Passed me by and bullied ahead and in
Agitation I followed and when the
Light turned red I caught up by using the

Margin of the street to bypass cars — we
Had words we tangled and I fought rested
Fought — wearing my overlarge helmet — and
He escaped but the police took me and

Questioned the American cowboy and
Somehow they concluded I was harmless.

I already knew
harmony is the way and
anger is poison —
I recognized in a snap
I forgot everything.

So the Zen master in the *dharma* hall
Told the monks about listening to the
Words of his Zen master in the *dharma*
Hall but his time in the monastery

He said amounted to eating rice and
Going to the latrine and his main job
Was managing a slobbering water
Buffalo that went where it wanted and

Did what it wanted and whether he tried
The kindest entreaties or whipped like a
Mad man he couldn't control the beast and
It wandered into the gardens but then

In the midst of wholehearted effort it
Became pacific and obedient.

As the obdurate
buffalo was his ego
he finally saw through —
a transparent companion
a connection everyday.

Japanese make a fetish of cuteness
For children and a TV show featured
The adventures of Thomas the train and
His friends Oliver and Percy who have

Faces on colored engines and my kids
Watched so I scootered in Kyoto looking
In toy shops and department stores for the
Dozens of characters and Trevor the

Tractor was hard to find so I stopped in
Towns while returning from *Hosshinji* and
Found him as the perfect prize after a
Week of meditation and I don't know

Whether I or my children enjoyed the
Trains most but I discovered the toy stores.

The clerks in toy stores
and the monks at the temple
saw me differently
in my rainy poncho gear —
I came for different reasons.

Continents

Angus

As a handsome youth with dark hair he's not
Remarkable but the photo has a
Story — he's just come to America
From Australia and I wonder what

The photo does to those of us who knew
Him as my father appears very much
Like me or my brother at that age and
He's full of youthful open confidence

As we know the story of his life of
His family his ministry the journal
He founded — we know the bitterness the
Courage and the triumphs no one else could

Comprehend and each of us remembers
Differently as each knew him separately.

It's a small circle
of people capable of
comprehending the
photo's reverberating
depth as only we knew him.

Hazel was his sister's name and dad said
She had a hard life as her husband was
A brute character and my dad would gaze
At the photo of her youthful smile and

Her profusion of hair and I can see
A touch of family resemblance as
The enthusiastic innocence and
Openness communicates happiness

But you can't tell by seeing the photo's
Eight decades old and between them was a
Steamer that traversed the Pacific from
Australia to America when such

A trip seemed irrevocable as dad
Left behind his family and homeland.

In youthful photos
of my vanished family
of a faded world —
I can sense optimism
And eager exploration.

His smile and youth are very appealing
As the uniform and the cocked hat could
Indicate anyone going to a
World War and his name is Billy Spargo

And he looks like any teenager does
Though I know on a bombing raid over
Germany he was killed because my dad
Told me — as they were friends in Australia —

And the burst of tears surprises as dad
Said he died because the Allies needed
A show of strength — the smile disintegrates
Distance and time and decades later my

Dad mourned — and as my dad has also died
The story of the photo is passing.

Once the people go
the stories of their photos
go along with them —
we are left with artifacts
but the memories are gone.

I just assumed if I went somewhere else
I would have an adventure so seeing
A map seeing Galveston Island in
Texas on the Gulf of Mexico it

Differed so much from Minnesota so with
My bicycle I got on a bus and
Went south and discovered how to be a
Waiter at a sea-food restaurant and

When riding on the ten-mile seawall I
Flew with the wind but when I turned it was
Hard pedaling all the way and I found
Being alone in a small boarding room

Was very much like being alone in
A dorm room and that I remained lonely.

Being at home is
a process a tempering
of the head and heart —
I don't have a clue until
accepting difficulty.

A song from thirty years ago brought to
Mind the time I wanted much more from life
While I was lonely and useless and lost
So I got on an airplane and went to

Japan thinking I could change myself by
Going someplace else — just as I left for
Santa Barbara and Galveston for a
Season before returning — but this time

Was different — I was sober — my head was
Clear — my emotions were capable of
Adapting — and I was very lucky
To be experiencing teenage angst

While I was only twenty-four-years-old —
And the song encapsulates the spirit.

Briefly I worked at
Jump Academy teaching
children and mothers
English singing dancing and
ignoring inhibitions.

While walking on the street I noticed the
Differences between the shops and office
Buildings and looked for landmarks that I could
Remember because I came yesterday

Knew nothing and was afraid I couldn't
Find the way back to the guesthouse and I
Saw a restaurant that appeared familiar
Got a table and a menu that I

Carefully scrutinized that the waiter
Kindly turned right side up and luckily
They had a glass case displaying plastic
Representations of menu items

To point at but it was a gamble — I
Saw how it looked but how did it taste?

The Japanese
have arms and legs —
they walk like me
went in doors looked out windows —
everything else was strange.

The City

How little emotion the faces of
The passengers on trains show how alone
I am traversing the crowded station
And there's a silence distinguishable

From the quality of sound between us
As if we were each untouchable — how
Indistinguishable are the faces
Contrasting so much with the brightness of

Recognition when I happen upon
A friend in passing — such are the comforts
Of a friend in a city as there's a
Shattering of anonymity as

A smile returns a smile as a friend has
Friends and introductions open the doors.

It's the density
of the population the
possibility
that anyone I could meet
could introduce anything.

I was riding on the train from Kyoto
Where I was staying to Osaka where
I worked and the three hundred yen for the
Ticket was the last of my money as

It took a while to get steady work and
I was going to ask for an advance on
My paycheck from the language school where I'd
Just been hired and as I hadn't money

For the return trip I'd arrived at the
Point of decision I'd been dreading and
The determination was out of my
Control as I was coming to the edge

Of fearful reality preparing
To face any eventuality.

I have gratitude
for experiencing raw
reality as
I've been learning how to
face the unpredictable.

The rules of sumo are simple within
The straw ring the wrestlers face off and
At a signal they rise up from a crouch
And grapple and if one touches any

Part of the body besides his feet on
The sand he loses — and my favorite
Was Mainoumi because he was so
Small going against Konishiki the

Jiggling five hundred pound Samoan
Who didn't move much while Mainoumi
Circled maneuvered manipulated
Leverage as Konishiki was leaning but

Mainoumi disappeared beneath him —
And Konishiki wobbled and toppled.

Sumo's a sport of
strength and weight and technique
of slapping gripping
maneuvering footwork and
of balancing behemoths.

Pioneer Park

A chill touches my cheeks and burns — a car
Passing touches my ears with sound — the sun
Rising touches my eyes with waves of light —
And the city of Stillwater as seen

From a bluff with homes nestled within slopes
With a view of the river valley with
The lamps on the street lit as their timing
Has not caught up with an earlier dawn

Touches my memory with traces of
The boy in me walking downtown to stores
That no longer exist — and I breathe and
The air touches my lungs — and I embrace

And am being embraced by a city
I had left behind but have returned home.

A circle clearly
appears to have an inside
and an outside too
but it's only a thin line
artificially imposed.

So I was in the square in Paris just
Before Notre-Dame Cathedral after
A year of schooling at Oxford having
Scored well with the teachers and being a

Young man with prospects for success who was
Free of responsibilities and yet
I couldn't be happy — now here you are
Accomplished graduated prepared to

Be an engineer a young man with no
Obstacles except that you're unhappy —
Is the world to come so threatening so
Imponderable it's hard to begin

Or is misery merely a habit
You must overcome? You will find a way.

Unfortunately
I'm not able to give you
exact guidance as
in matters of the spirit
we each have our own puzzles.

As if I were trying to sneak a look
At his cards to see what he's doing he
Holds back and won't communicate how he's
Considering his options what he wants

To do what he thinks he's capable of
Becoming — it's time that he makes his way
That he determines a direction and
I know he doesn't have to get it right

There's wide latitude — it's not a lifetime
He's planning just the first few steps and then
He may reconsider readjust and
Change course but how can he know what's best for

Him without testing his abilities
And discovering how the world responds?

Because he's done it
because he's reconnoitered
possibilities
a father may guide his son —
but the son may be stubborn.

Being in a place where a person was
Makes the separation more poignant and
Who am I to complain as didn't I
Get on a bus to Galveston Texas

And take a plane to Osaka Japan
And didn't my parents wave goodbye and
And didn't they watch me depart to an
Uncertain fate thousands of miles gone

And haven't I been wondering when you
Would take a worthy direction but now
I realize emotions can become
Mixed as your courage is inspiring

As you're behaving just as I did but
Part of me I've found wants to keep you near.

How can I complain
of my son's emulation
as Joshua has
decided to go northward
up to Juno Alaska?

Philadelphia

Jocelyn

You were resisting in Pioneer Park
Pouting and refusing to walk on a
Summer afternoon as resolute as
A toddler with a bulging tummy

Could be bereft of her container of
Water that I forgot so I scooped you
Up and we proceeded home — today you're in
Graduating robes at Moore College of

Art and Design in Philadelphia
Which is far from home with a degree that's
A gamble the schooling will be useful
As we have encouraged you to become

As creative as possible because
Your talent deserves opportunity.

The conveyance of
emotional subtlety
comes naturally
in faces you create so
experience carefully.

Philadelphia is a trip as the
Streets are trashy and everywhere grit is
Accumulating and no one has the
Wherewithal to deal with it and I feel

Up against the Philadelphians as
They project boundaries of wariness
Aggression indifference and sometimes
Curiosity and courtesy as

I met a woman who bakes cakes with all
Her heart and she stayed quiet with her guests
While she was watching and she responded
With happiness to words of well-earned praise —

Things may go wrong in Philadelphia
And Philadelphians are quite prepared.

Philadelphians
are sizzling with tension
each impacting each
other unpredictably
so I have to be wary.

City Center Philadelphia

In the sky the glass and steel towers are
Leveraging geometrical beauty
With psychological impact on the
Passersby walking on the streets as I

Imagine meeting at the top discussing
Important decisions amidst the blending
Of shining clouds and blue sky even as the
Multitudes mingle anonymously

Below as cranes are lifting workmen and
Busses taxis and people are flowing —
She's attractive and he's intriguing — and
Corporate shops and ethnic delis are

Interspersed and there's a lot to see and
Everyone comprehends variously.

Exclusivity
and prestige are impressive
but I know enough
to gaze upon surfaces
with curious amusement.

The Rental

The luxury and oversize were not
Choices I made as the ordinary
Vans weren't available so for the same
Price I took the black and silver thing we

Dubbed "The orca" afraid of getting it
Scratched in Philadelphia as the streets
Were clogged the highways congested and the
Navigation system treacherous when

On the way to the airport pressed for time
We found ourselves boxed within an alley
Behind a university waiting
For forty containers of trash to be

Dumped in a garbage truck — as I relished
The unanticipated adventure.

I was piloting
a star ship by the parked cars
decorating streets of
Philadelphia afraid
of a second's misjudgment.

Cottonwood Poems

Within the several days when the leaves of
The cottonwood are finally down and
Most of the daylilies and hostas have
Withered and the pines have shed their twigs when

I rouse myself to stoop and pull and cut
And rake and bend and gather and stuff and
Bag and carry and I move from task to
Task with enthusiasm finally

Once I've overcome the dread beforehand
And on the morning after I'm happy
To have honorably crossed the threshold
Of winter again with the soreness and

The battered fingers and the tidy yard —
I've earned a respite before the snowfall.

Winter approaches
in an overwhelming surge
a massive onslaught
just over the horizon
incontrovertible chill.

If I were a squirrel a cottonwood
Would be my principality would be
My house of many mansions and I would
Scramble over every inch and I would

Grasp the craggy bark and scamper up as
Far as I could go and then I'd clamber
Out precariously along each limb
To find a favorite vantage point but in

Time I'd find my customary byways
I'd establish a civilized routine
Of eating here and washing up there at
The appropriate time of day and I

Would find a very special crook where I
Could curl up to dream my squirrel dreams.

The yammering and
yelping of the frustrated
dogs below would be
hilarious but I'd keep
an eye open for the hawks.

To watch the swaying of the dangling limbs
Of the cottonwood tree in a slight wind
Through a pane of glass streaking with the drops
Of rain and to see beyond the many

Limbs of other trees dispersing their so
Delicate endings in the air with buds
Visible within the grey sky for me
Is to notice the strangeness of this place

That from the ground the trees grow and from the
Horizon the sun rises and we have
Rain today and we're on the cusp of spring
Again and I have the eyes to see the

Changing seasons and the lungs to breathe the
Fresh air and the heart to be receptive.

A giraffe and a
hippopotamus and a
rhinoceros are
especially strange beings —
but so is a cottonwood.

It's a half-grown leaf and one of thousands
On the cottonwood tree and this morning
It's illuminated and flickering
As the sun and a brisk wind has caught it

Just so and all of the long dangling limbs
Of the tree are swaying and so the wind
Is stirring the leaves with a sounding that's
Arising in spring — and as I live in

A neighborhood of trees everywhere there's
The rocking motion and the swelling and
The dissipating sound of the wind in
Trees I haven't heard since autumn and the

Rhythm of the rising and falling wind
Is as soothing and welcome as ever.

The birds have returned
and yesterday I noticed
their singing before
dawn as I had forgotten
their morning celebration.

It would have drained if it were the normal
Accumulation of spring water but
The pooling around the drain persisted
Within the basement and as we behaved

As usual an odoriferousness
Arose signaling something awry so
We called the drainage guys who discovered
I was the responsible owner of

A broke sewage pipe that came across the
Roots of the cottonwood tree — and a ditch
Ten feet deep from the house all the way to
And underneath the street would have to be

Excavated or else I could keep my
Broken pipe and build myself an outhouse.

Before the sewage
pipe broke I didn't know I
could afford to pay
the thirteen thousand dollars
parceled out in monthly checks.

The problem is I'm not evading the
Confines of myself as the chatter in
My mind is trivial habitual
Inconsequential so I gaze at one

Of the cottonwood's dangling limbs high
In the air and notice the absence of
Wind and the half-grown leaves are heart shaped and
They are accompanied by sprays of seeds

Just emerging and behind tendrils of
The tree the sun is burning right through a
Cloud so brightly I close my eyes and my
Lids are red with light and then the cloud is

Gone — all I have to do to clear my head
Is indulge my senses and stop thinking.

Suddenly the sun
goes behind the craggy trunk
and the leaves light up
while the dangling tendrils
and the trunk become darker.

The leaves are dipping up and down in the
Rain pattering on the cottonwood and
The limbs are swaying slightly and the bark
Is darkening with water in craggy

Grooves — Nicholas White decided to take
His life this week — he was mentally ill
Kind and a talented pianist on
An edge who could not be present enough

With his friends — and we gathered and have done
Rituals and are left with questions as
There's music and gentle motion in the
Air in gray brown shades in a milky sky —

It seems the rainy day is like a veil
I want to pull aside to see better.

Could we have
rescued Nicholas White
with better words
with more compassion
and what do we do now?

If the leaves of the cottonwood tree were
Bells there'd be jubilant music this morning
As there's a steady breeze and they're turning
In unison all of them up and down

The long dangling tendrils numbering
Maybe thousands and if you've noticed how
The sunlight sparkles on a river how
The light flickers there is the same flashing

As leaves catch the light momentarily
And they are flickering and swaying in
A gentle wind with the pristine freshness
Of spring and just as I enjoy seeing

The undulating river in sunlight
I am rejoicing with the flowing tree.

The cottonwood
is a mixture of
elements people
considered vital —
earth water fire and wind.

I'm sensitive to dust that causes my
Airways to constrict so it's difficult
To breathe and for twenty years I've dreaded
When the yellow leaves of the cottonwood

Are finally down because on that day
It's my job to dispose of them and I've
Mulched with my mower for twenty darn years
Always bringing on an asthma attack

Having to take in the medicated
Mist of the nebulizer afterwards
But this year I discovered the wondrous
Qualities of a rake and lawn bags for

Preserving equanimity and for
Revealing I'm not too stubborn to learn.

I always believed
in the simplicity of
the mulching mower
but I've discovered a rake
is marvelously simple.

One at a time or in groups in a gust
Of wind the yellow leaves flitter from my
Cottonwood tree — the tallest tree in the
Neighborhood — and I've often thought its girth

And height magnificent even sublime —
And yet every year it dumps a load of
Yellow nuisance on the grass and two years
Ago its roots rearranged my sewage

Pipe that cost thirteen thousand dollars to
Replace — so if a guy could resent a
Tree I have every reason to but I've
Grown accustomed to the ritual at

The end of autumn — of picking up the
Droppings of this imperturbable tree.

It's a natural
monument with a nasty
habit of shedding
twigs and branches I have to
pick up continuously.

Politics

Imagine standing on a battlement
Of a castle in chain mail with a sword
At your side keeping watch through a cold night
While trying to stay warm — recreate the

Training necessary the courtesies
Expected of the network of people
In the levels of hierarchy and
The presence of stone and steel and mud and

Snow and wind and fire and chickens and how
Difficult would it be to heal a wound
How would the joints of the body age and
What would be the spectrum of opinion

About what happens when a person dies
And what encouragements would be useful?

And how differently
would the moon and stars be felt
without a certain
measure of size or distance —
a wonderful mystery.

Imagine the presence of a King in
His fortress while you are surrounded by
His knights with their weapons within arms
Reach realizing He has your life in

Hand to take or preserve according to
His benefit — Imagine being the
King and the necessary precautions
Of instilling fear and fostering love

Of the Kingship so as to govern with
A prospect of success — and imagine
The meaning of the law serving the King
With the purpose of obedience and

Imagine the weight of the fear in the
Moment as His Eminence calculates.

Authority and force
submission or rebellion
with blades or bullets —
someone exercises law
and someone proclaims justice.

On Tuesday morning on television
As the first tower was burning I watched
The second airliner explode into
The second tower and the newscasters

Immediately thought of Osama
Bin Laden just as I was thinking of
Him and so within our American
Consciousness the potentiality

Of an attack from a beautiful blue
Sky was realized in a shock many
Years later we're so reluctant to grasp
Willingly — the heart of our culture is

Vulnerable — in the name of Islam
Some people intend relentless warfare.

Seeing a woman
concealed in a burqa
Westerners receive
a striking lesson —
some people think differently.

As civilized as a sword can make us —
Wasn't it a cultural achievement
To fold the steel in layers and forge it
With a hammer and anvil and hone the

Blade to lethality to inscribe it
With vows of victory and to wield it
Requires a warrior's training to
Surpass the enemy's might in battle

And all to no benefit without a
Supporting ethos infusing courage
In the warrior? As civilized as
We may be in the midst of savagery

Haunting the human animal forcing
A defense of gentle accomplishments.

And there are methods
for instilling compassion
and benevolence
in the midst violence
in the human dilemma.

"Unbeliever" and "heathen" are words used
To separate people into high and
Low regard and it's impossible to
Use the words and not assume a moral

Posture even in opposition to
Their meanings and to say "bigot" about
Someone is often to be a bigot
Oneself as people do divide into

Groups and oppose each other and I see
The categories we create and
How allegiance easily affixes
To a body and I see boundaries

Are enforced mutually by fear and
So is it surprising that we bicker?

Without gentleness
without assimilation
without sympathy
differences are dangerous
bickering is endemic.

Hate

It's used to justify the marshalling
Of power and it's seductive because
It's rooted in fear and with sharp reason
As people do divide against themselves

By history culture ethnicity
And religion and it's as easy to
Hate a group as an individual —
Hatred and war are endemic — and the

Associated politics confusing
As the pursuit of truth and ideals are
Deformed in the process — thus producing
Divisions within a population —

And whatever petty meanness exists
Discovers an empowering excuse.

A mesmerizing
message and a call to arms
in the name of God
is powerful impetus
beyond conciliation.

They live through their wits and expertise and
They know much more than most of us do as
They have years of experience and the
Networks of contacts knowing who has the

Money and what are the intricacies
Of the laws and what are the processes
Necessary to move the direction
Of government — they are politicos

Consummate insiders — who understand
Bureaucracy and taxes and leverage —
And they know how to mount a crisp line of
Attack or defense as the case demands —

And we can't do without them but also
In a free country they can't be trusted.

Intelligence is
necessary for the game
but the nation needs
honest politicos and
genuine public servants.

How human it is to be caught up in
A political discussion and find
Myself becoming agitated and
An advocate for a point of view as

America is sophisticated
And powerful and the nation contains
Energized factions organizing to
Manipulate mass consciousness and so

The news is filled with events that trigger
Emotional responses from people
Who are captured for different reasons by
A point of view and unfortunately

It's much too easy to be passionate
About issues beyond our influence.

It's human to be
caught in a net of power
politics as the
spectrum of opinion is
established and divided.

When the President gives a speech before
Both houses of Congress on the state of
The union in the glorious chamber
Of the capital building his words are

Greeted with standings or sittings and with
Enthusiastic or tepid clapping
Precipitating a partisan slant
Or reflecting the popularity

Of a banality — but mostly it's
Palaver to placate the gullible
And everyone knows it — and it would be
A forgettable exercise except

Washington is a fulcrum and the world
Is moved by people who are devious.

As Washington is
where taxes are divvied and
bureaucrats govern
and influence is traded —
while justice is haphazard.

Opinions vary and disagreements
Proliferate and try to cajole the
Uninformed to profess his ignorance
And try to surpass your righteousness to

See the complexity of politics —
And behind the arguments is the cold
Reality of people grasping for
Themselves and thereby taking sustenance

From the clueless — I see with the lens of
Limited government and liberty
And I advocate for the adoption
Of disinterested ideals and

The cultivation of clarity to
Eviscerate the specious narratives.

Don't be deceived by
rhetoric and illusion
as politicians
are very good at twisting
vulnerable emotions.

I sometimes notice I allow myself
To be determined by the way things ought
To be and I focus on an outcome
And a driving force arises pushing

Me to bring about the way things ought to
Be and whether it's my relationships
Or the management of the business or
The immigration policy of the

Nation I do become quite stubborn as
I can't see another way being good
Enough — and then obstacles arising
Require thought and sometimes it's important

To practice relaxation to expand
My range of vision — or to persevere.

The frustration and
aggravation are questions —
do I need to push
am I seeing correctly
and is it worth the struggle?

I don't know how anyone could be here
Watching the political scene with a
Dog in the fight and not have anger and
Fear arising as it's about who wins

And loses — and the loss is real or seems
So — and as I share with my *sangha* and
Discuss the *dharma* and believe that hate
Does not diminish hate but love does — and

As I cherish the direction and can
Almost penetrate the boundary of the
Ethereal — I am living in the
Realm of passions and of gain and loss and

However much my intellect absorbs —
I don't know how to liberate my heart.

I believe that words
alone are insufficient
that the *dharma* points
the way to liberation —
and liberation happens.

I'm lucky to have found ideals for the
Most humane and liberating form of
Government that are culled from history
Economics experimentation

And *The Federalist Papers* on the
Motives of humanity with a view
Of natural law — but if I encounter
Unscrupulous opposition and if

My reputation is diminished and my
Livelihood is jeopardized I wouldn't
Be surprised — because the advancement of
Ideals is risky — but I'm lucky because

I've also entered the *Buddha* way and
I know how to practice and be quiet.

Judeo-Christian
Greco-Roman ideals
may liberalize
much of society — and
meditation is lovely.

Racism does exist and it's a fear
Of strangers based on appearance and it's
An ancient hatred abiding in the
World but the word "racist" is used as a

Smear of groups of people whose hearts and minds
The politico shouldn't judge — as he
Is attacking masses of strangers he
Doesn't know based on their appearance — and

He is cultivating resentful minds
Among his followers — redirecting
Hatred — perpetuating precisely
The same evil he is accusing his

Targets of because he's doesn't desire
Reconciliation he wants power.

Today's politics
involves manipulating
mass consciousness to
delegitimize targets
depersonalize people.

In a "half-faced camp" a shed with three sides
They lived not much better than bears in a
Cave because that's the best Thomas could do
Hewing a shelter from the woods with an

Ax and saw — they arrived after fourteen
Days in an oxen caravan to a
Fork on the Sangamon River to a
Place without obligations and to a

Site where Nancy his mother would die from
Milk sickness where Abraham learned to do
Sums of arithmetic by writing on
A wooden shovel and shaving it off —

He had a year's schooling but he absorbed
The Bible and Robinson Crusoe.

Weighing his words and
speaking dispassionately
Abraham Lincoln
would present his arguments
sincerely and precisely.

Abraham Lincoln

He was moved with compassion for the slaves
Declared the nation must choose slavery or
Freedom when none wanted to see the truth
He knew the choice could not be evaded —

Thoughtful and grave with a far-away gaze
Burdens settled on him as he became
The master of himself and of many
Hot-tempered men contesting Civil War —

The north fought to preserve union and law —
Not to free slaves — Lincoln understood the
Temper of his people knew not to waste
The slaughter of soldiers so he waited

Until emancipation could succeed —
He was the only one fit for the job.

Sadness troubled him
compassion moved him to lead
strength sustained him through
thousands of battlefield deaths —
may he be honored always.

Blunderbuss

It's ornate on the hill overlooking
The valley just below the historic
Courthouse and the memorial for those
Of the First Minnesota who died at

Gettysburg with its thick layering of
Brown paint on its carriage and with its dense
Coating of black the cannon seems a bit
Unreal — but I'm impressed by its size and

Its design — because there's nothing graceful
About it because it's meant for slaughtering
Soldiers and — perhaps it's the distance in
Time and from a battlefield that creates

A ceremonial vibe — but to me
It represents ruthless brutality.

The bronze statue of
the union soldier with his
bayonet fixed is
advancing — and concealing
the terror he must have felt.

If I don't surrender belligerence
I won't find the balance I need — if I
Don't acknowledge my defiance I won't
Escape my frustrations and self-pity —

Because people and situations are
Like mirrors reflecting back to me the
Attitudes and emotions I carry
And every justification even

Justified reasoning if taken with
Truculence rebounds to punish me — so
How do I function within a world that's
Divided into warring factions when

With good intentions I believe I'm called
To be political and to persist?

I want to be as
articulate confident
and determined as
possible — and I also
want to avoid bitterness.

Myths and Dreams

It came from the ancient Greeks whom we don't
Understand — from a poet's telling of
A warrior's long journey home — and the
Obstacles he defeats with persistence

Resourcefulness trickery — and it seems
A violent phantasmagoria —
When intelligence and brutality
Were admired — and often survival

Was hand to mouth — and so Odysseus
Lulls the Cyclopes into drunkenness and
Puts out its eye with a burning stake and
His companions aren't eaten — and I can

Imagine horror and despondency
Turned to euphoria and victory.

We don't control the
inspiration of dreams of
the visitation
of primal reality —
visceral memory.

Daedalus was a such a magician the
King demanded his allegiance but as
Daedalus was also particular
He would not serve — so he fashioned wings of

Wax and feathers for himself and his son
To flee from Crete — and he advised the youth
Not to fly too near the sun because the
Design was fallible and required

Careful use — but because Icarus was
Young and impetuous he could not be
Reasonable with a gift of divine
Power — so he flew too high and the wax

Melted and the wings disintegrated
As Daedalus watched and could do nothing.

As Icarus plunged
into the sea Daedalus
realized the cost
of divine inspiration —
without due humility.

With satellites compassing the earth and
Ubiquitous video and instant
Communication there's no place beyond
Reach anymore as long as a person's

Properly plugged in to modernity —
As the quicksilver god Hermes has been
Left behind a swift jetliner gasping —
As we view the earth below a layer

Of clouds — and yet Hermes is also
A prankster snickering at security
Protocol and the interminable
Lines necessary at the airport as —

No matter how quick we are we can't leave
Behind our baggage of tomfoolery.

As mysterious
as the trivial squabbles
on Mount Olympus —
human rationality
is incomprehensible.

It's ideal and imagination
Couldn't improve the white gypsum sands of
New Mexico within the dome of an
Empty sky — though it might be better with

No one here because the soundless beauty
Evokes the presence of perfection as
If this were a high Olympian
Plain and people aren't compatible here — as

Trudging in the white sand is difficult —
Marching to a goal exhausting — and each
Step an exertion — but companions are
Encouraging — and the sacred air is pierced

With laughter and the sterile atmosphere
Is overcome with raucous commotion.

Aspirations for
perfection reside within
imagination —
experience is messy —
and laughter divinity.

I looked at the castle of glass in the
Sky and considered how it would be to
See the people below as so many
Minuscule dots — and I imagined how

Daily life would go amidst the clouds and
Light wondering whether I'd settle in
A funk with thunder — and exuberance
With the sun — or would I become enmeshed —

Acting and reacting with the people
I was cloistered with — just as we do on
The ground — but I believe the rituals
And the traditions in the great hall would

Instill a sense of privilege — and a fear
Of losing status — and being sent down.

The impression of
the dream lingered long enough
for me to grasp the
difficulty of letting
go of prestige.

We had a destination and a goal
And I was driving as quickly as I
Dared between the looming towers of the
City at night because the woman the

Friend and I were propelled and excited
As every second was precious and my
Sensations were keen — and then the alarm
Sounded and I woke — and just like a wave

Receding I lost my connection to
The intricate vibrant reality
Of that world — and I grieved for my friends as
Our shared mission was dissolving — because

It was a vital drive interrupted —
And I rose and returned to normalcy.

I love the
the blue sky of
consciousness —
and I don't understand
dreams.

The everyday sky with a few drifting
Clouds is a façade I take comfort in
While the reality is visible
At night — in the black vastness that's lit with

Stars — that's impossible to comprehend —
And however embroiled and compulsive
I may be as I make my choices with
People during the day when I drift off

Into the phantasmagoria of
Dreams I'm in an altered reality —
As I'm leaving the safety of harbor —
As I'm entering the swelling tumbling

Roiling rolling of the mournful ocean —
And I am most passionately alive.

I'm presented with
puzzling scenarios
poignant emotions
unpredictability
forgetfulness when waking.

If I were to play with symbology
I'd create myself as a coin — and on
One side would appear my face with the sun
Representing my doings including

My habits emotions accomplishments
And all my aspirations — but on the
Other side would be the moon and a
Sailing ship amidst a sprinkling of

Stars — as an acknowledgement of spirit —
As I lay asleep sizzling with dreams
Reverberating with experience
Of all the lives I've lived — or perhaps I'd

Be communing and taking guidance from
The animating and invisible.

The days are for my
goals and accomplishments —
but my dreams at night
represent my being — and
mysterious consciousness.

Who crossed the threshold of hunger and fear —
And did it happen haphazardly or
Suddenly as individuals were
Inspired and became leaders of tribes —

Who began the primal impetus of
Craving understanding of creating
Explanations for the sun the moon the
Stars the seasons birth and death — because there

Was an awakened consciousness on the
Earth — as human beings became aware
Of the mystery of our presence — and
We needed purposes worthy of our

Suffering — and though our ignorance has
Diminished aren't we a questing people?

I know about the
millions of supernovas
billions of light years —
but how on earth do I grasp
purposes worthy of life?

Stone Masters

See the ingenious industry in
The transportation cutting and setting
Up of the gargantuan stones and see
The meticulous necessity of

Following the movements of the stars and
Sun for the channeling of the rising
Sun trough single gates — and appreciate
The grace and artistry of the design —

And marvel at their ambition — that a
Neolithic people could comprehend
The vast forces of the universe — and
That with mighty inspiration they would

Expend their precious energy in an
Expression of connection at Stonehenge.

And why did they carve
such monumental faces
on Easter Island
and painfully set them up
under the moon sun and stars?

From precisely this point — from nowhere else —
Does this moment flow to infinity
Beyond limits of imagination
Enfolding every possibility

As I am sitting at my desk looking
Out the window seeing the cottonwood
With just a few surviving yellow leaves
With the blue sky as a background as I'm

Considering what I should do with my
Time this afternoon as there are things that
Need doing and things that can wait but for
Now I'm immersed in the words "the one bright

Jewel" that are used to described this moment
As a moment of surpassing freedom.

This moment is a
culmination of
flowing circumstance
and a point of departure
if I can summon presence.

Indra's Net

Each is radiating the sunshine and
Each is absorbing the resplendence of
The others and to gaze within one is
To see the reflections of all — so the

Blending emanations of the King of
Heaven's net of jewels is a mythical
Explanation of our elemental
Situation from the point of view of

Light and spirit and thought woven in one
Source from which we descend into a life
On earth — I don't know why we struggle so —
It's hard to make sense of so much here and

I can't imagine what life in other
Dimensions would be like — I'm not meant to.

How elemental
to be dazzled by sun —
it's too much
to withstand the blaze
without the shade of trees.

You are a drop of dew on a spider's
Web and I am too as we connect on
Gossamer threads and every person is
A drop sharing connection on the web —

As the sun rises and light penetrates
You and you reflect me and I you and
We reflect everyone and each of us
Contains a reflection of each other —

So much of how I've come to be reflects
So much of how you've come to be reflects
Very much how each of us has come to
Be through the gossamer connections with

People — shining dewdrops in the morning
Sun — I cherish my connection with you.

I don't want to be
and I could never have been
separate alone
within a meaningless void —
I need you for me to grow.

Whether you are an impediment or
Disappointing or even obnoxious
You've been helpful — because the frustration
Of dealing with you is energizing —

And whether I'm righteous or mistaken —
Your opposition is clarifying —
Because sometimes I'm able to admit
Being right or wrong is provisional

And temporary within a flux of
Circumstances — and sometimes I notice
How self-appraisal can resemble a
Fun-house mirror — and I do recognize how

Reckless behavior creates a hall of
Mirrors — and so I need your perspective.

My eyes aren't enough
and I need you to balance
my perspective — as
this world is confusing and
we need to cooperate.

Were it better you be a person who
No longer exists for me within my
Way of thinking and feeling — so I
May go about my business without the

Hindrance of wanting to know where you are
And what you're doing — as was often my
Pattern of yearning — as I could not stop
Thinking about you — but now you seldom

Come to mind and I've dispersed my passions
Into habits free from an unhealthy
Dependence on you to a wide open
Array of friends with whom I've learned to be

As light as a feather — because now I
Feel at home within my head and heart?

No — I could not have
found a home within me if
you hadn't helped me
on the way — so I want to
remember you with kindness.

Heart Sutra

The cardinal in the apple tree is
A splash of crimson surrounded by snow
On the branches the ground the roofs of homes
On a misty day as I'm pondering

The words of the Heart Sutra saying form
Is emptiness and emptiness is form —
Form doesn't differ from emptiness and
Emptiness doesn't differ from form — so

Is the red bird in a white landscape a
Phantom and is my joy a delusion
Is everything and nothing the same thing
Like a bubble that has already burst?

There is a cardinal in an apple
Tree and I do enjoy seeing the bird.

The bodhisattva
Avloketeshvara
says wisdom exists
before knowledge and
she heeds suffering.

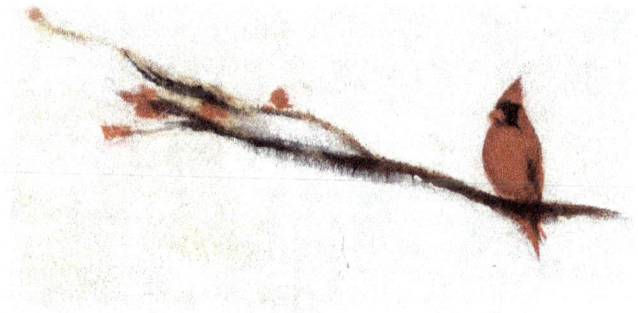

If dissatisfaction is woven in
The fabric of human life and if I
Experience suffering by grasping
For the unobtainable and if there

Is a way out of suffering if I
Follow the Buddha's eight-fold path then how
Can I understand the Heart Sutra that
Says there is no dissatisfaction and

No end of dissatisfaction either
There is no eight-fold path and even the
Buddha never existed because form
Doesn't differ from emptiness then how

Do I escape emptiness and how do
I come to terms with my dissatisfaction?

The Buddha said
an unborn and
undying presence
is woven in
everything.

If my existence arises with thought
If I'm constructing the world with my thought
Then what should I think when appraising the
Heart Sutra that empties the eyes the ears

The nose the tongue the skin and the mind and
How should I behave when the Heart Sutra
Also empties the seen the heard the smelled
The tasted and the objects of my thinking

As if my memory were delusion
As if my habits were ephemera
As if my conscience were an illusion
As if my dreams were nugatory and

This vibrant moment is only a trick?
Then maybe the sutra is just crazy.

From the sky
flakes of snow
are circling and
I'm celebrating
their presence.

If I were losing
my marbles in
dementia as
I was emptying
would I struggle?

— *Tekkan*

www.ingramcontent.com/pod-product-compliance
Lightning Source LLC
Chambersburg PA
CBHW052103070526
44584CB00017B/2311